Wisdom Speaks

Hearing Her Voice In A Noisy World

Kathy J. Smith

9562 Woodside Circle
Grand Blanc Mi 48439

Wisdom Speaks

Hearing Her Voice In A Noisy World

Kathy J. Smith M.A., ADN

ISBN 978-1-61529-174-8

Copyright © 2016 by Kathy J. Smith

Vision Publishing
1115 D Street
Ramona, CA 92065
1 800 – 9 – VISION
www.booksbyvision.com

No part of this book may be reproduced in any manner without the written permission of the author except in brief quotations embodied in critical article of review.

All scripture is New American Standard unless otherwise stated.

Acknowledgements

I would like to acknowledge the many people that have helped make this book possible.

First and foremost, to God my Father, to him be the glory. To Jesus Christ, my brother and Savior, and to the Person of the Holy Spirit, the true voice of Wisdom.

Thank you to the staff of Vision International for encouraging me, and a special thank you to Dr. Stan DeKoven for his support and willingness to review and edit this book.

A special thank you to my friend, Dr. Cathy Guerrero who has been a source of support and inspiration to me along with the beautiful women of Lifebuilders.

My friend and prayer partner, Erma Kummerer, who has spent endless hours supporting me in prayer and helping to proofread this book. You may be thousands of miles away in the physical sense, but you are still there and support me daily. Thank you.

To the church family at the Toledo Tabernacle and their wonderful pastors, Dr. Calvin Sweeney and Pastor Christine Sweeney who were the first to hear this content in June of 2016. Thank you for inspiring me to write this book.

Dedication

I would like to honor both of my parents, Joe and Dorothy Smith, who have always believed in me and stood at my side. I would also like to honor Drs. Tal and Dee Klaus who have been like family to me since I moved to California. Talk about the voice of wisdom. Wisdom speaks through each one on a consistent basis. This book is dedicated to each of you.

Foreword

Like many others I have been in pursuit of wisdom for my life, although at times we can become so busy or involved that we overlook the voice of wisdom. Wisdom calls to us as the voice of reason in a cluttered and noisy world, yet we tend not to recognize it. When we ignore wisdom and take things into our own hands we can misunderstand and easily become misaligned.

Proverbs 3:5 (Amplified Translation) Lean on, trust in, *and* be confident in the Lord with all your heart *and* mind and do not rely on your own insight *or* understanding.

We need wisdom's voice to navigate through deception as well as the storms of life, to bring us into a safe harbor. One of the scriptures that I use as a wisdom compass is found in Proverbs 24:3-4 (New Living Translation) Any enterprise is built by wise planning, becomes strong through common sense and profits wonderfully by keeping abreast of the facts.

Wisdom is necessary to planning. As it has been said, "If we fail to plan, we are planning to fail." We must apply that wisdom known as common sense, and continue to watch how wisdom works as we honestly look at the facts.

As Voltaire said "Common sense is not so common." Kathy's application of scripture and analogies illustrates how God works through life lessons to bring strength and courage to our lives.

I met Kathy several years back and was immediately impressed because she encompasses courage and strength, along with gentleness and tenderness. She is a champion who obediently follows God with her "whatever it takes" attitude to accomplish her God-given purpose and mandate. Her talent, courage and passion have opened doors, allowing her voice to impact many.

Kathy has been on a journey of discovery, unearthing the treasure of wisdom's voice to share with us. She has navigated many life challenges, which caused her to press into the place of recognizing the voice of wisdom and having the courage to apply wisdom by faith.

Kathy lays out wisdom principles that she was challenged in, and also how to apply God's word for wisdom. From overcoming limiting mindsets, to facing fear, to transitions across the nation and stepping on foreign soil- leaving comfort and convenience to obey God's voice.

Wisdom Speaks clearly explains how to discern wisdom, even through pain and discomfort. Wisdom's voice gives us the courage to stand up when others lie down and curl up in fear. The voice of wisdom breaks open hidden plans through revelation releasing the constrained.

Jeremiah 33:3 (Amplified Translation) Call to Me and I will answer you and show you great *and* mighty things, fenced in and hidden, which you do not know (do not distinguish and recognize, have knowledge of and understand).

Wisdom Speaks is a profound resource for those who want to know and understand the voice of wisdom, discern between external voices and the internal voices of emotion, and conquer the temptation to stay in the familiar.

Enjoy your journey as you learn how *Wisdom Speaks*.

Dr. Cathy Guerrero
Pastor Regency Christian Center International
CEO/Founder Life Builder Seminars

Table of Contents

Acknowledgements 3
Dedication 4
Foreword 5
Introduction Wisdom Speaks 9
Chapter 1 It is a Noisy World Out There 13
Chapter 2 Which Voice Has Your Ear? 21
Chapter 3 Voices, Voices, Everywhere 31
Chapter 4 The Unconditional Promises of God 41
Chapter 5 New Season, New Territory, New
    Navigation Strategy 47
Chapter 6 Is Your Filter Clogged? 55
Chapter 7 Do You Hear Her Now? 59
About the Author 63
Recommended Resources 64

8

Introduction

Wisdom Speaks

Proverbs 1:20 Wisdom shouts in the street, she lifts her voice in the square. NASB

No one sets out in life to fail. No one puts failure on their bucket list. No one wants to be known as a failure. Yet a certain amount of failure is inevitable. Failure is not who we are, but merely an unfortunate situation through which we must walk; it is a circumstance, not an identity. We <u>can</u> choose to make set backs and mistakes a mere stepping stone to a successful and prosperous future.

Thomas Edison was said to have failed at least 1000 times before success was realized in the invention of the light bulb. He did not consider the many setbacks as failures, but rather, each failed attempt took him one step closer to a solution. He grew in knowledge with each set back, and the wisdom he gained in the process led him to success.

What if Lucille Ball would have quit after being dismissed from drama school for being too shy? What if the Beatles would have given up after the Deca recording studio turned them down because they said guitar music was on the way out? What if Walt Disney would have taken the criticism of a newspaper company to heart when they fired him for having no imagination and no original ideas? What if Michael Jordan had thrown in the towel and pursued other interests when he was cut from the high school basketball team? What if Paul Young, the author of the best seller, *The Shack*, gave up after his book was refused by 26 different publishing companies?

Not one of these people gave up after initial failed attempts. Just because we make mistakes, perhaps we have even failed a time or two, that does <u>not</u> need to be the final epitaph engraved upon our gravestone. Rather, it merely means we have learned what did not work. That takes us one step closer to our inevitable end, success.

Mistakes must not hold us back. Rather, we can choose to use the information we have learned to catapult us into our expected future. We can choose to use the wisdom we have gained to move us toward success. We can choose to learn, even from our mistakes. **Failure is only failure if we choose to quit.**

Don't make that choice, do not give up. Don't quit. Take the wisdom and the knowledge you have gained from your mistakes and keep moving forward. If it is something God has placed in your heart, then success is inevitable, that is, **unless** you throw in the towel.

Wise counsel is like honey on the bread of life. Wisdom is sweeter than the words of the crowd. In all that you do, seek wisdom. Solomon said, the principal thing is wisdom. What is wisdom? Wisdom is the art of being successful in life.

Using knowledge and understanding to make wise judgements, and then acting upon that wisdom to create a plan for life, we can reach the desired goal. We can complete our course, we can finish the race, we can hear, "Well done my good and faithful servant…"

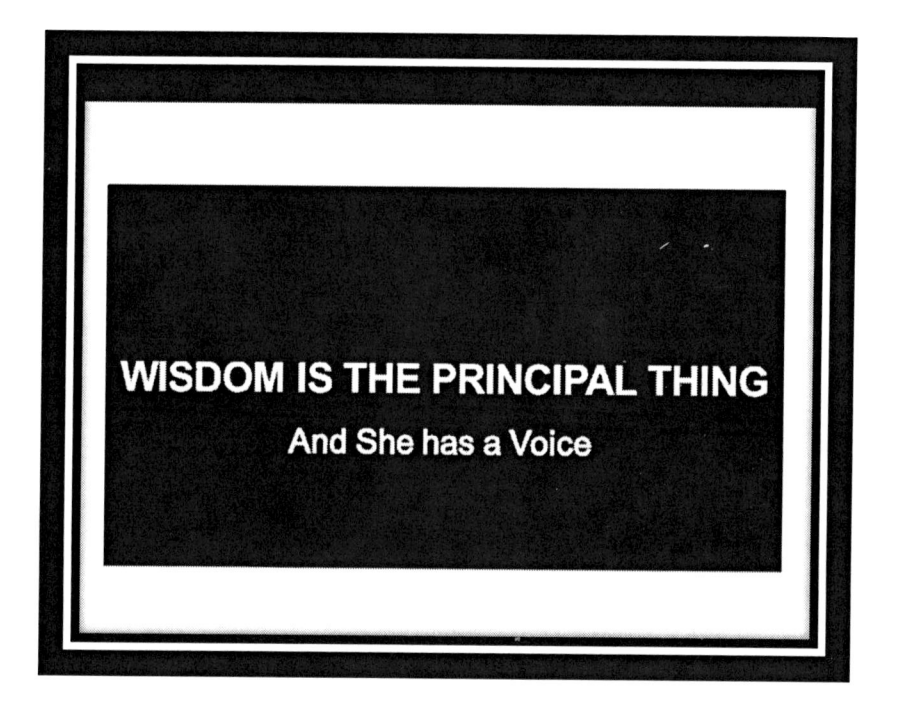

WISDOM IS THE PRINCIPAL THING
And She has a Voice

***1 Corinthians 14:10** There are, it may be, so many kinds of <u>voices</u> in the world, and none of them is without signification.* KJV

Chapter 1

It is a Noisy World Out There

There are many voices in the world. Although many other versions translate the word *voices* as languages, the King James Version is more true to the original Greek word in this verse...it means voices or sounds.

I am reminded of a country song that recently became a hit, the title of the song is, "Noise." The song was recorded by Kenny Chesney. As one listens to the lyrics, the subject of noise, which includes voices, is addressed. In many ways, he is speaking a similar truth; in the world there are many sounds and many voices, in his own modern day vernacular he sings:

In part,

> "Wrecking balls, downtown construction
> Bottles breaking, jukebox buzzing
> Cardboard sign says the lord is coming
> Tick, tick, tock
> Rumors turn the mills back home
> Parking lot kids with the speakers blown
> We didn't turn it on but we can't turn it off, off, off
> Sometimes I wonder how did we get here
> Seems like all we ever hear is
>
> Noise
>
> Yeah we scream, yeah we shout 'til we don't have a voice
> In the streets, in the crowds, it ain't nothing but noise
> Drowning out all the dreams of this Tennessee boy"

As the song reiterates, all we ever hear is noise. We did not turn it on, but we can't turn it off. The noise, and the multitude of voices in the streets and in the crowds, can drown out the sound of our own voice and thoughts.

Another verse from this song reads:

> *"Every room, every house, every shade of noise*
> *All the floors, all the walls, they all shake with noise*
> *We can't sleep, we can't think, can't escape the noise*
> *We can't take the noise, so we just make*
>
> *Noise"*

Noise, as this song suggests, threatens to drown out our hopes and dreams. We find ourselves surrounded on every side, day in and day out, with the sound of noise, and the sound of a multitude of voices.

1 Corinthians 14:10 states that all voices are significant, but we need to understand that some voices will lead us astray; they will lead us down the wrong path. We cannot come into agreement with every voice that we hear. There are many voices in the world.

I am reminded of the scene at a local fair or an amusement park. Walking down the midway there is booth after booth of games that one can play to win a prize. At each booth a barker calls to entice us to play the game. Wisdom tells us that we cannot respond to each one that calls, they would merely rob us blind for a couple of stuffed animals.

Wisdom has a voice; but discerning her voice can be challenging. There are so many other voices. There are the voices of our parents, children, or a spouse. There are the voices of employers, friends, neighbors, politicians, teachers and government officials. They vie for our attention and place a demand on our time, our energy, and our emotions.

Some have our best interest at heart, others have more personal agendas. They seek to be heard. They desire to influence; they desire to impart their own wisdom and knowledge, they desire to challenge one's sense of reason. Some wish to make a withdrawal from your person; your time, energy, emotions, or resources. If they are making a withdrawal, what is it, if anything, they have deposited? Do they take without giving, or do they give without taking? Or is the relationship mutually beneficial?

The Voice of Reason

Reason has a voice of her own with which she speaks. She may borrow the voice box of your mother, teacher, or employer, but nevertheless she speaks through whichever vessel that she can.

Have you never been confronted by someone who wanted to talk sense into you? This confrontation may have been triggered by a disagreement with an opinion you voiced, or by one of your decisions or actions. They often begin with, you <u>must</u> listen to reason... what you are doing is not right. The voice of reason can be a weighty opponent indeed.

Proverbs 28:26 *The righteous is a guide to his neighbor, But the way of the wicked leads them astray.*

In the world there are many sights, sounds, and voices.

Paul, in Acts 21:12 – 14, found himself being advised by friends who loved and cared for him.

> *"When we had heard this, we as well as the local residents began begging him not to go up to Jerusalem. Then Paul answered, "What are you doing, weeping and breaking my heart? For I am ready not only to be bound, but even to die at Jerusalem for the name of the Lord Jesus." And since he would not be persuaded, we fell silent, remarking, "The will of the Lord be done!"*

The counsel of friends was just and reasonable. Their intentions good, they cared. The voice of reason spoke through the voice of friends. They warned him, do not go to Jerusalem; yet Paul refused to heed the voice with which reason spoke. Was he wrong? Of course not, he heard the voice of wisdom speak and so he responded.

In Numbers 13 and 14 twelve spies were sent into the promised land by Moses and told to return with a report. Ten spies returned with a discouraging report, but two came back encouraged. Hearing the fear of the ten spies, the people rebelled and refused to go any further. The voice of reason had spoken and they listened.

Reason's Voice may Contradict What You Know in Your Heart

I have heard the voice of reason speak many times, and often what she says makes total sense, and I go with it. But then, there are times that **she contradicts something I already know in my heart, something spoken by another voice.**

One such occasion was when I first began contemplating international ministry, and even more recently, when I was preparing to go to Austria. A person close to me, one who was concerned about my own personal wellbeing, called to speak to me. We had a conversation regarding my decision to go to Austria to teach. They advised me that it was not safe and there was no significant purpose for me to go to a foreign land to teach. After all, there were plenty of opportunities in the states, and even in California to do ministry. There are plenty of people who need help and teaching right here in the good old USA, and there is no reason to travel abroad. Besides, it costs too much money.

I knew that the voice spoke their own truth, and had arrived at their opinion through facts that could be substantiated. They spoke the truth as they knew it. The voice of reason had made her case. However, I had already heard another voice; one that spoke directly to my heart.

She spoke her truth, and what she spoke was of far greater significance than anything the voice of reason had to say. It was the voice of wisdom that had called to me to go to the nations and teach. I had heard her speak, and knew in my heart, that I needed to go.

We are confronted on every side, from without and within, by voices vying for our attention.

In a multitude of counselors there is safety (Proverbs 11:14, 15:22, 24:6), but we must have the wisdom to know the difference between good counsel and bad. We cannot respond to every voice that speaks. Some speak out of ignorance; others seek fulfillment of their own agendas, not ours. We need to filter the sounds that we hear, to know the one with which wisdom speaks.

If one wanted to watch the news they may turn to Fox or CNN. If they wanted to follow sports they would turn to ESPN. If they wanted to learn more about cooking, perhaps the Food Network would be helpful. Where do you turn to hear the voice of wisdom?

> **Isaiah 30:21** *Your ears will hear a word behind you, This is the way, walk in it," whenever you turn to the right or to the left.*

Wisdom has a voice. Do you have an ear to hear what she speaks to your heart?

There are many voices in the world, which one has your ear?

Proverbs 4

Hear, O sons, the instruction of a father, And give attention that you may gain understanding,

For I give you sound teaching; Do not abandon my instruction.

When I was a son to my father, Tender and the only son in the sight of my mother,

Then he taught me and said to me, "Let your heart hold fast my words; Keep my commandments and live;

Acquire wisdom! Acquire understanding! Do not forget nor turn away from the words of my mouth.

"Do not forsake her, and she will guard you; Love her, and she will watch over you.
"The beginning of wisdom is: Acquire wisdom; And with all your acquiring, get understanding.

"Prize her, and she will exalt you; She will honor you if you embrace her.

"She will place on your head a garland of grace; She will present you with a crown of beauty."

Hear, my son, and accept my sayings And the years of your life will be many.

I have directed you in the way of wisdom; I have led you in upright paths.

When you walk, your steps will not be impeded; And if you run, you will not stumble. Take hold of instruction; do not let go. Guard her, for she is your life.

Chapter 2

Which Voice Has Your Ear?

Voices are everywhere, but which voice do you hear? Which voice has your ear? In the first nine chapters of Proverbs, King Solomon speaks of three specific voices that he claims are vying for our attention. One he tells us to embrace and the other two, avoid.

We have all heard of the Wisdom of Solomon, he is known as the wisest father to have ever lived in human flesh. The wisdom that he possessed was partially imparted by his own father King David and his mother Bathsheba. However, the wisdom with which King Solomon has been credited far exceeded the wisdom of his biological parents. He asked God for the wisdom to rule a nation, and God graciously granted his request.

Wisdom is a valuable commodity. Typically it is passed from one generation to the next as an inheritance of great value and a priceless legacy. The legacy of wisdom that King Solomon had for the generations to come, and specifically for his son Rehoboam, was great though not followed. There is much that we can glean from his advice; in essence it is the wisdom for living a successful life.

King Solomon embraced wisdom as the key to success. While Wisdom has a voice, as he so eloquently wrote, so does the strange woman. Let us see what he has to say about her first.

The Strange Woman

To deliver you from the strange woman,
From the adulteress who flatters with her words;
That leaves the companion of her youth
And forgets the covenant of her God;
For her house sinks down to death
And her tracks lead to the dead;

*None who go to her return again,
Nor do they reach the paths of life.*
Proverbs 2:16 –19

For at the window of my house I looked out through my lattice, And I saw among the naive, And discerned among the youths A young man lacking sense, Passing through the street near her corner; And he takes the way to her house, In the twilight, in the evening, In the middle of the night and in the darkness.

And behold, a woman comes to meet him, Dressed as a harlot and cunning of heart. She is boisterous and rebellious, her feet do not remain at home; She is now in the streets, now in the squares, And lurks by every corner. So she seizes him and kisses him And with a brazen face she says to him: "I was due to offer peace offerings; Today I have paid my vows.

"Therefore I have come out to meet you, To seek your presence earnestly, and I have found you. "I have spread my couch with coverings, With colored linens of Egypt. "I have sprinkled my bed With myrrh, aloes and cinnamon.

"Come, let us drink our fill of love until morning; Let us delight ourselves with caresses. "For my husband is not at home, He has gone on a long journey; He has taken a bag of money with him, At the full moon he will come home."

With her many persuasions she entices him; With her flattering lips she seduces him. Suddenly he follows her As an ox goes to the slaughter, or as one in fetters to the discipline of a fool, until an arrow pierces through his liver; As a bird hastens to the snare, so he does not know that it will cost him his life.

Proverbs 7:6-23

The strange woman is spoken of frequently in the book of Proverbs, and is one that we all want to avoid. It tells us that she is an adulterous woman, a harlot, one who does not honor her covenants with man or God. In other words, she is immoral. She knows how to use flattering language to entice others, but once entrapped, there is no turning back. Verse nineteen says that none who go to her return again.

The scriptures tell us that by their fruit, we shall know them. She may boast of wonderful things, and use enticing words to do so. She may at surface level appear desirable and attractive, but the fruit she bears is death. Do you remember the fig tree that Jesus cursed? Why did he curse a tree that had no fruit when it was not the season for it to bear fruit? (See Matthew 21:18-22 and Mark 11:12-14, 19-25)

The scripture tells us it was full of leaves. This may not be significant to you unless you know that fig trees are not to grow leaves until after the fruit appears. The fact that this tree had leaves boasts of fruit it did not have. From a distance, one would think it was fruitful, but when you come close the truth is known. No fruit.

Solomon warned against falling for the strange woman's flattering words and enticing behavior. She boasts of a blessing to those who partake of her fruit, but her fruit is anything but blessed. Her motive is destruction. If she can divert one's attention from the appropriate course and capture their ear, the trap will be set, making death inevitable. Not all things are as they appear, as with the fig tree.

Did Paul not discern the spirit behind the voice of the woman slave in Acts16:16-18? He became annoyed and he ordered the spirit to come out of her. We must use our discernment to avoid wrong influences. When in doubt, check it out.

What fruit does the personified voice truly bear in the end? Is it the fruit of sin and death, or joy, peace, and harmony? Does it bear the fruit of repentance and eternal life or destruction? You be the judge! While we are not to judge one another, we are to inspect the fruit and discern spirits. For a more in depth study of the characteristics of the strange woman please refer to Proverbs 7 in your bible and the corresponding commentary of your choice.

The Voice of the Foolish Woman

Solomon warned of another woman, her name is Folly, and she has a voice with which she speaks. The question is who will listen to what she has to say?

> ***The woman of folly*** *is boisterous, She is naive and knows nothing. She sits at the doorway of her house, on a seat by the high places of the city, Calling to those who pass by, Who are making their paths straight: "Whoever is naive, let him turn in here," And to him who lacks understanding she says, "Stolen water is sweet; And bread eaten in secret is pleasant." But he does not know that the dead are there, That her guests are in the depths of Sheol.*
>
> **Proverbs 9:13-18**

The woman Folly speaks, and she speaks in a very loud manner and her brashness reveals her character. She is boisterous, naïve, and knows nothing; she lacks wisdom. Those who have an ear tuned to what she has to say will foolishly follow after her.

Allow me to paint a picture in your mind of a small group of teenage boys with time on their hands, and mischief on their minds. They notice a couple of other boys, a bit younger and impressionable and so they approach.

"You two look bored; want to hang out with us? We were just about to have a little fun, and you are welcome to join us." And so the unsuspecting boys join the others. "Why not?" says one boy to the other. "We don't have anything better to do."

So the boys tag along, but they quickly discover that the fun includes stealing a car and going on a joy ride that will take them somewhere they never intended to go, jail. Once lured into the trap, they lacked the wisdom to know how to exit. So they went along with the others, all the way to jail.

You do not have to be young and naive to be caught in a foolish trap. Many an adult has befriended the wrong person and found themselves caught in a situation that was far from the intended path. Men or women, who unsuspectedly found themselves in an abusive relationship, an illicit affair, a business deal that turned out to be less than legal; these are all examples of listening to the wrong voice.

Pastor Andrew Hopkins of San Marcos, CA shared in a recent sermon, "When you listen to the liar you get steal, kill, and destroy as your fruit." He went on to say, "What you listen to becomes your belief, and what you focus on you empower." In other words, if you listen to lies and focus upon them, you empower them. If you listen to the truth, you then empower the truth to produce fruit. This is a profound statement and exemplifies what we are discussing in this chapter. What voice are you listening to and what fruit does it bear?

Furthermore, how can we avoid listening to the wrong voice and being caught off guard? Allow me to answer with yet another question. How do you learn to tell the difference between a counterfeit $20 bill and the real thing?

You must study the real one until you know it inside and out, without a doubt. Once you know what the real thing looks like, a counterfeit is easy to spot. If you know the voice of wisdom intimately, then the counterfeits will never have a chance to catch you off guard. Solomon spoke of wisdom,

> *"Do not forsake her, and she will guard you; Love her, and she will watch over you.*
>
> *"The beginning of wisdom is: Acquire wisdom; And with all your acquiring, get understanding.*
>
> *"Prize her, and she will exalt you; She will honor you if you embrace her.*

Proverbs 4:6-8

The Voice with Which Wisdom Speaks

The third woman of which Solomon wrote about in the first nine chapters of Proverbs was the voice of wisdom. How can we begin to embrace her as Solomon suggests? How can we develop an intimate relationship with the woman he describes?

In the beginning…

Every story must have a beginning. The story chronicling the search for Wisdom has a beginning; the obtaining of Wisdom has an origin. Solomon said that the beginning of wisdom is rooted in the fear of the Lord. (Proverbs 9:10) While this fear should not predicate cowering in the corner shaking in fear, it does suggest a reverent respect and honor for God the Father who created us.

What other hints did Solomon leave for us? "Fear of the Lord is the beginning of wisdom but knowledge of the Holy One is understanding." Knowledge that leads to understanding takes the relationship far beyond that of a casual acquaintanceship. One can possess the knowledge that they have a new neighbor across the street without having understanding of who they are as a person. What are their likes, dislikes, attitudes, or opinions? Understanding with knowledge is acquired through relationship.

Adam had more than a casual relationship with Eve. He knew her because he had a relationship with her. Their relationship lead to intimacy and as a result of this, Adam gained understanding of who she was. We do not suggest this was merely a physical relationship, but one in which each shared their thoughts, cares, concerns, and desires with one another.

Having a relationship with God that bears the fruit of under-standing requires more than just an awareness of his existence, but rather a process of bonding and intimacy that allows for knowledge of God's character to be acquired. While we may know who he is and fear him in reverence, knowledge that leads to understanding can only be acquired through an active and ongoing relationship in an intimate manner.

Wisdom is personified as a woman, one who has a voice with which she speaks; but wisdom is more than just a voice. Wisdom is a person, and is the person of the Holy Spirit.

Wisdom offers an invitation to all that will listen, she says, "Come, eat of my food and drink of the wine I have mixed." (Proverbs 9:5)

> *Wisdom has built her house,*
> *She has hewn out her seven pillars;*

Proverbs 9:1

Wisdom has built her house; she has prepared the feast and set the table. She sends out her maids to invite the guests. All are encouraged to enter in to her house and partake of the meal that she has prepared. Wisdom is available to all who are willing to listen. James tells us,

> *But if any of you lacks wisdom, let him ask of God, who gives to all generously and without reproach, and it will be given to him.*

James 1:5

What is the house that wisdom has built; I suggest it is God's kingdom here upon the earth. And the pillars which support the structure? Various scholars have differing opinions on what the seven pillars represent. Some say they are seven attributes of the Holy Spirit as seen in Isaiah 11:2, others reference the attributes found in Proverbs 9:12 – 14.

Another teaching that has become quite popular in the past few years was first introduced by three men in 1975, after having visitations by the Lord with similar messages. The men were Bill Bright, founder of Campus Crusade, Loren Cunningham, founder of Youth With A Mission, and Francis Schaeffer of L'Abri fame.

More recently others such as Lance Wallnau and Bill Johnson have also taught on the concept of seven cultural mountains that impact nations and affect society at large. They are:

1. Church/Religion
2. Education
3. Family
4. Government
5. Media
6. Arts
7. Business/Finance

We will learn more about the voice with which wisdom speaks in upcoming chapters. But for now, it is important to understand that she does have a voice, and she speaks to those who are willing to listen. Recognizing the voice of wisdom is key to living the successful life, as Solomon stressed over and over again.

Although Solomon stressed the concepts of embracing wisdom and turning away from the Harlot and Folly, he did not always follow that instruction in his personal life. It tells us in Chapter 11 of 1 Kings that King Solomon loved many foreign women.

In his later years his heart was turned away from God to serve the gods of his foreign wives. Is it any surprise then that the son that he had so faithfully instructed in the way of wisdom would eventually turn aside from the path of wisdom to listen to others?

Peer Influence Split a Kingdom

Rehoboam was 41 years old when he ascended to the throne of his father, King Solomon. (His reign is described in 1 Kings 12 and 14:21-31 and in 2 Chronicles 10-12)

Because Solomon turned away from the statutes of God to serve the foreign gods of his wives, God was displeased. As a result, he was determined to split the kingdom. Out of respect for David, he did not execute his plan while Solomon was still alive. But after Solomon's death, Rehoboam, his son, would have the kingdom ripped out from under him. He was left with nothing more than one remnant tribe.

The People Speak but the King Won't Listen

The people, along with Jeroboam came before King Rehoboam to speak of the heavy labor and high taxes which King Solomon had imposed upon them. They sought relief from this excessive burden. Rehoboam told them to return in three days for his answer.

Rehoboam consulted the wise men that had advised his father, and they counseled him to do as the people wished and speak kindly to them. He refused their counsel however, choosing to listen to the voice of his peers instead. Rather than lightening their burden, he determined to increase it. Therefore the people rebelled and the kingdom was split. The people who left chose to make Jeroboam their King.

The actions of King Solomon,
spoke more loudly than his words.

In his latter days,
he strayed from the instruction of his father,
and from the Voice of Wisdom,
and his son did likewise.

Chapter 3

Voices, Voices, Everywhere

In the last chapter we discussed the three voices identified by King Solomon in Proverbs. They were the Strange Woman, Folly, and Wisdom. There are however, many different voices in the world. While we can't possibly name them all, we can identify a few.

For instance, the voice of reason; we spoke of this voice earlier. A few others are: the voice of the world, the voice of peers, the voice of experience, the voice of our emotions, and the voice of the past. Each speaks loudly at times, and must be responded to.

Noises from the world are often so loud
We cannot hear ourselves think.

As previously stated, demands are placed upon our time by friends, family, and employers. Sometimes it seems that we become so busy, we can do nothing more than put out the fires. The squeakiest wheel usually gets the oil first. Let us talk about a few of the voices that we may hear.

The Voice of the World.

This is perhaps not one definitive voice but the collection of many voices from around the world that speak on behalf of society as a whole. They may come together in agreement to speak to a specific topic or issue of mutual concern. For instance, one might say that the voice of the world cries out against the atrocities that are being inflicted upon innocent people in escalating numbers of acts of terrorism across the globe today.

The Voice of Reason.

The book of Esther is a perfect example of the voice of reason versus the voice of wisdom. Think of it, had Esther listened to the voice of reason she and her whole people group would have died! By natural means, Esther had no hope of saving her people, but by God's means she became queen and turned the heart of the King. Esther was God's undercover intelligence. She was the one woman rescue team on a covert mission to save a nation.

Another example from biblical history is Noah. How absurd he must have looked building the ark. He was nowhere near water and at the time it had not yet rained. Just imagine what his friends, neighbors, and relatives must have been thinking and saying. The voice of reason would have said, "This is ridiculous." We know that another voice spoke directly to his heart, and because he heard and responded, his family was saved.

Again we can look at Abraham. His wife was far past the age to bear children; but Abraham had heard the voice of wisdom speaking to him regarding the multitudes he would father. Did he listen to reason or the voice of wisdom? You know he ignored the voice with which reason would speak to believe the word wisdom spoke.

When the time came to sacrifice, Abraham took Isaac obediently and placed him upon the altar. Reason would have said, "Are you crazy?" But wisdom told him that God would supply, and he did.

Reason is not always bad. Sometimes the voice of reason makes total sense and I go with it. In fact, there are many times when the voice of reason speaks wisdom. However, when reason speaks differently from the voice of wisdom in your heart, **choose wisdom**. The voice of reason may come from others, or from within. When it comes from within, it is better known as self-talk.

An important study was done on the topic of self-talk by Psychologist Ethan Kross. In an article appearing in Psychology

Today[1] May 4th, 2015, Kross reported becoming interested in the topic of self-talk beginning in the spring of 2010. He recounts driving through Ann Arbor, Michigan when he passed a red light. He addressed himself at the time saying, "Ethan, you idiot!" He took notice that he addressed himself by his first name. He questioned why he would refer to himself by his name, and what significance that might have.

Over the course of the next few months, he noticed others who did the same; not the least of which was LeBron James as he spoke to television crews regarding his decision to leave the Cleveland Cavaliers to play for the Miami Heat. He is reported as saying, "One thing I didn't want to do was make an emotional decision, I wanted to do what was best for LeBron James, and to do what makes LeBron James happy."

His curiosity was heightened at this point regarding the use of one's first name instead of a pronoun. The interest led to a series of experiments involving self-talk and how it affects our performance in life.

I quote the article by Pamela Weintraub here, "By toggling the way we address the self—first person or third—we flip a switch in the cerebral cortex, the center of thought, and another in the amygdala, the seat of fear, moving closer to or further from our sense of self and all its emotional intensity. Gaining psychological distance enables self-control, allowing us to think clearly, perform competently. The language switch also minimizes rumination, a handmaiden of anxiety and depression, after we complete a task. Released from negative thoughts, we gain perspective, focus deeply, plan for the future."

Self-talk, or the voice of reason, can be beneficial in alleviating the pull of emotions in our decision making and makes it possible to hear the voice of wisdom more clearly. It can also be the voice of irrationality. Positive, rational self-talk can be a valuable tool to self-

---

[1] https://www.psychologytoday.com/articles/201505/the-voice-reason

motivation and rehearsing past victories. I know that many think that if you talk to yourself you are crazy, but in actuality the direct opposite is true.

Negative self-talk can be destructive to your self-esteem, but positive self-talk will help you bolster your own confidence and cut through the red tape that emotion would bind you with. So, the next time you or someone you know are caught talking to themselves, know this, they may be very wise indeed.

The Voice of Experience.

Many times teachers speak from the voice of experience. Experience can give one the authority to speak and teach with wisdom about a specific topic. However, when one becomes rigid in thinking and not open to new ideas, it can have the opposite affect. Fluidity of thought is necessary for creative juices to flow. Only then is advancement and transformation possible. When one is inflexible in their thinking, they are closed to new ideas and the ever flowing creativity of God. One must have the qualities of humility, patience, meekness, and a teachable spirit before they can become qualified teachers in the eyes of God.

The voice of experience may say, this is the way we have always done it. The voice of experience may say, this always happens in this situation. When an experience is negative in nature, it can create a sense of hopelessness.

A pattern of similar experiences, either negative or positive, can create strong mindsets. The voice of experience can create inflexibility and closed thoughts. When emotions from an experience are strong, the voice of wisdom will likely be muted in the hearer's ear. (More on the voice of emotions in a few minutes.) Some mindsets that result from repetitive negative experiences are a poverty mindset and a victim mentality.

The child who is continually picked on by peers, family, or others may accept and expect that type of treatment as inevitable. They may carry the negative mindset with them into adulthood, where it can continue to do damage and hinder God's plan for success. Unless the cycle is broken, they will learn to expect the worst from most all situations. The same negativity may result from the state of lack. Someone born into poverty may accept that it is their lot in life, and stop trying to find a way to break free from the pattern.

Success can also hinder flexibility and transformation. Those who have been successful with a specific product, service, system, or just life in general, may become disillusioned with a sense of having arrived. They think, as long as I continue to do it the same way, it will continue to be effective and will continue to deliver for me in the future. This is a dangerous mindset; it dismisses God given creativity and hinders future advancement. It produces stagnant thinking, and stagnant thoughts that stink up our future.

How do we avoid the stagnancy that produces unproductive and unwanted thought patterns? We must change our mindset. When we change the way we think about our circumstances, it becomes possible to break the pattern of negative thinking and begin building bridges to a successful future.

Inflexibility and negative mindsets create roadblocks. Choose to rethink how you approach a potential obstacle in the road. You can choose to stop dead in your tracks and remain forever defeated, or you can choose to utilize the roadblock to catapult into your future and your expected end.

The Voice of Our Own Emotions.

In a post by Kris Vallotton dated July 10, 2016 he stated this about feelings or our emotions.

5 things you need to know about feelings:

    1- Feelings don't always tell the truth.

2- How you feel is not how you are!

3- Valuing your feelings, without letting them determine your decisions is maturity.

4- If you change your mind your feelings will follow.

5- True love is an act of your will, not an emotion you feel.[2]

Feelings don't always tell the truth, but the voice of our emotions can become quite loud and demanding, especially when we have been hurt or become angry at some injustice. Whenever we react with our emotions, rather than responding with wisdom, we are in danger of making mistakes in judgement that we will later regret.

Making choices and decisions based upon wisdom, and not our emotions is the key to successfully navigating through difficult circumstances. Sometimes it is necessary to table important decisions until our emotions have had the opportunity to die down. Only then can we think clearly enough to make wise choices based upon the voice of wisdom speaking to our heart. Sometimes our emotions shout so loud, we cannot hear wisdom speak.

Do not make key decisions in life based upon emotions alone, but wait for that still small voice with which wisdom often speaks. She will not lead you astray, but rather into a peaceful solution.

> *Who among you is wise and understanding? Let him show by his good behavior his deeds in the gentleness of wisdom. But if you have bitter jealousy and selfish ambition in your heart, do not be arrogant and so lie against the truth. This wisdom is not that which comes down from above, but is earthly, natural, demonic. For where jealousy and selfish ambition exist, there is disorder and every evil thing. But the wisdom from above is first pure, then peaceable, gentle, reasonable, full of mercy and good fruits, unwavering, without hypocrisy. And the seed*

---

[2] Posted on Facebook July 10th of 2016 by Kris Vallotton Ministries

whose fruit is righteousness is sown in peace by those who make peace.

James 3:13 -18

The Voice of the Past

Don't allow a blast from the past to rob you of your future. Don't allow future trials and tests do that either. Some events and circumstances seemingly brand folks with a false identity. They can mistakenly adopt their situation or circumstance as who they have become. We must not identify with what we have been through, nor what has been done to us. We must find our identity in Christ. All else is merely a lie, or at least incomplete.

Some may have had cancer; but that is not their identity. Some people may have been born into poverty, but it is not their identity; it is simply something they have been forced to walk through. Some may have been victimized, but it is <u>not</u> their identity; we are all victors in Christ. No matter where we have been, no matter what we have experienced, or what we will go through in the future; it is not an identity but a circumstance. Our identity is in Christ.

The Voice of Peers

Those close to us can become very influential in helping form our opinions and guiding our decision making. I do not want to dwell on this voice too much, but I do wish to counsel you to use wisdom in deciding who you allow close to you and who you have counsel you.

Solomon in Proverbs 1:5, says this,

> *A wise man will hear and increase in learning, And a man of understanding will acquire wise counsel,*

Not all counsel is wise, as Rehoboam discovered when he allowed his peers to influence him. As a result of this error, the kingdom was split. Choose your friends wisely, and adhere to counsel from those whose judgement you can trust.

In all your ways acknowledge Him,
And He will make your paths straight.

Proverbs 3:6

> A wise man will hear and increase in learning,
> And a man of understanding will acquire wise counsel,
> Proverbs 1:5

Chapter 4

The Unconditional Promises of God

For as many as are the promises of God, in Him they are yes; therefore also through Him is our Amen to the glory of God through us.

2 Corinthians 1:20

Many are the promises of God, and he is not a man that he should lie. That which he has promised, he is also able to fulfill. I might add, that the plan and purpose for which he created you is still on the table as well, that is, <u>if</u> you want it.

For I know the plans that I have for you,' declares the L<small>ORD</small>, 'plans for welfare and not for calamity to give you a future and a hope.

Jeremiah 29:11

The sound of life and the sound of the many voices we encounter each and every day, often drown out the sound of everything else, including wisdom's voice. It muffles the sound of our own thoughts, hopes and dreams; the God given dreams we have had for the future. Life has a way of getting in the way, and calling us up short; but the plan and purpose for which you and I were created, does still exist. Romans 11:29 says:

- *The gifts and the calling of God are without repentance. KJV*

- *God's gifts and his call are irrevocable NIV/NASB*

- *For God's gifts and his call* **can never be withdrawn.** *New Living Translation*

I prefer the New Living Translation here; it states that God's gifts and his call can never be withdrawn. Underline the word **NEVER**. Does that mean except, if I mess up and sin against God then I can no longer fulfill my purpose, the purpose for which I was created? Does it mean except if I take a detour and venture out in a different direction of my own choosing perhaps? Does it mean that if I take the wrong path, I can never find my way back?

Let us look at the verse once again; *For God's gifts and his call can never be withdrawn.* The enemy would love to convince you that God's promise is conditional, but there is no condition set forth in this verse. Hence the emphasis I place on the word never. While God does not disqualify us, at times we disqualify ourselves.

For instance, there were twelve spies that went into the Promised Land but only two of them returned with a good report. Those two were the only ones to remain and go into to take possession of the promise. The others disqualified themselves through disobedience.

I remember a season in my life when I strayed from the path; it was a season of testing. My church home had some serious difficulties and eventually folded. This left a large number of people without a church, including me. Trying to fit into a new church proved to be arduous, and my whole family was hurt repeatedly, so finally we just gave up. We stopped trying to fit in and stayed at home. After all, I told myself, I can do my own church at home, right? There is a reason why the word tells us,

> *"Not forsaking our own assembling together, as is the habit of some, but encouraging one another; and all the more as you see the day drawing near."* **Hebrews 10:25**

We need to assemble together, to encourage one another, when one gets weak then another can lift him up. We were created for fellowship. We are stronger together. When the wolf wants to prey on the sheep, he works to get one isolated from the rest of the flock.

Alone the one sheep is defenseless. (Lev. 26:8, Deuteronomy 32:30 one can put 1000 to flight, 2 – 10000)

> *Two are better than one because they have a good return for their labor. For if either of them falls, the one will lift up his companion. But woe to the one who falls when there is not another to lift him up. Furthermore, if two lie down together they keep warm, but how can one be warm alone? And if one can overpower him who is alone, two can resist him. A cord of three strands is not quickly torn apart.*
>
> **Ecclesiastes 4:9**

Assembling with fellow believers makes us less vulnerable.

Once I had no church, I became an easy prey to the lies of the enemy. Pretty soon, my study time, prayer time, and praise time dwindled to almost nothing. Going without physical food makes the physical body weak and sickly, going without spiritual food and fellowship makes us spiritually weak and vulnerable.

If we allow it to, life can get in the way of our relationship with God. When this happens, it makes us an easy prey for the enemy. It looks like you can't get there (the fulfillment of your purpose) from where you are. This roadblock is merely an illusion, one meant to sidetrack you and get you off course. It is meant to destroy your hope and make you believe fulfillment of God's promise for your life impossible.

We have all heard that voice speaking to us, "Give up, there is no chance for you now, what you just did, what just happened to you, messed your life up so bad there is no hope." Your hopes and your dreams are off limits to you because of what just happened. It is a waste of your time to think you can complete the course now. The enemy will tell you anything to get you off course, to get you to give up.

Think of how Joseph must have felt. The young man in Genesis with the multicolored coat had great favor with his father and with God. He also had big dreams. God given dreams. Stuck in the bottom of a pit, and later sequestered in a prison cell for years on end, his dreams must have looked nearly impossible. Yet we know that the gifts and the call of God cannot be withdrawn. The dream of his youth came to pass, just as God said that it would.

Another youth named David was anointed King of Israel (1 Samuel), and yet it was many years before David saw fulfillment of the promise. He was forced to run for his life on several occasions, with Saul in hot pursuit. How impossible the dream must have seemed, yet we know it did come to pass; just as God said that it would.

God has a plan and purpose for your life too. If it seems totally impossible, that is ok. You are in good company, with Joseph, David, and Noah cheering you on (Hebrews 11). Their dreams from God looked a bit impossible to, but we know that God does not lie. The cloud of impossibility is just a smoke screen, it is not real. The truth is you can't fail. Don't believe the lie. It is merely an illusion. Trust God and you cannot fail.

I finally came to the end of myself and realized that my only hope was to be in a church body, and so I began rebuilding the relationship I had with the Lord. It was long overdue.

I searched for a church family that I could be a part of, and was successful in finding one. It was a long hard road back, but I am glad that I took the first step. It got easier with each step that I took from that point forward.

Yes, I had believed that I had disqualified myself from the gifts and the calling of God by not attending church, and by allowing my relationship with the Lord to become distant. While God's promise was unconditional, my actions separated me from his plan and purpose for my life.

The gifts and calling of God cannot be withdrawn; so I simply had to realign myself with his Word to fulfill them. I needed to renew my relationship, and get back up in the saddle again. God is good. He gives us second chances and more.

I would be lying if I said the journey was without difficulties. In actuality there were many roadblocks and hindrances in my future to overcome. Nevertheless, I had others at my side to help me through the rough places. When I felt weak, someone else would lift me up, and I did the same for them. Together we advanced both in our walk with God and with our advancement into the plan and purpose of God for our lives. Together we can establish the kingdom in strength and power.

It is important to be a part of a church family. The sound of wisdom's voice can be magnified in the company of likeminded people in search of the truth.

> For I know the plans that I have for you declares the LORD,
> plans for welfare and not for calamity
> to give you a future and a hope.
>
> Jeremiah 29:11

Chapter 5

New Season, New Territory, New Navigation Strategy

I remember learning to navigate in North Carolina and then in California. Navigation in those states is not what it is in rural Ohio, at least not the part of Ohio I come from. In Ohio, if I miss a turn, I just go to the next road, make three right turns and end up right back where I started. At that point, I am free to correct the navigation error and get back on track. It is not that simple in North Carolina or California. Making three right turns in California can land you really, really lost. I had to develop a new way of navigating to get me where I wanted to go. I had to rely on my GPS more than ever before.

New territory and new seasons in life may require reliance on new navigation techniques. Giving yourself time to acclimate to new surroundings and learning to adapt is the key to moving forward in new territories.

When I moved to North Carolina, I at least had my daughter and her family at my side to direct me where to go to find the best shopping, grocery store, and movie theater. I had someone to guide me when driving in heavy traffic in unfamiliar places. I remember the first time I tried to exit the street we lived on during rush hour.

I sat there watching the bumper to bumper cars passing by, waiting for the lines to let up enough for me to turn left across the traffic of this busy six lane street. Finally, my daughter said to me, mom, if you are going to turn left in the next two hours you will have to creep out into the center turn lane first, and then wait until the traffic coming from the other direction slows down enough that you can squeeze into the other lane.

Now that may sound funny to those of you accustomed to driving in heavy traffic, but I had not needed to use this driving technique before leaving Ohio. I also quickly learned not to use the turn right three times technique. North Carolina is not flat like Ohio. This was just the beginning of the adjustments I would need to make.

I was fortunate that I had a built in social network with which to spend my time, even though they were my daughter's friends, not mine. Making friends my own age was more difficult than I had anticipated it would be. I did find a few, especially toward the end of my year there. It was not an easy task. Even the culture in North Carolina was a bit different than Ohio. Little did I know that the adaption skills I learned that year in North Carolina would soon be put to the test.

A year after moving to North Carolina, the opportunity presented itself for me to move to California. This move would literally take me from one coast to another and from one culture to another. For a girl who grew up in farm country, flat farm country, and had lived less than thirty miles from where I was born for most of my life, this move was huge! The first step was to acclimate myself to the new surroundings.

With little more than a few boxes of books that were shipped ahead, and the clothing I could fit in my luggage and carry on, I transitioned to California. While the physical move may have been accomplished in less than one day, the transition in mindset has taken years. Acclimation and adaption is a process that takes time, and for some it takes more time than for others. I must admit it was *not* easy, especially considering the fact that I was sixty years old. There were more than a few tears shed along the way.

Once I arrived in California, I had to start over. I had to learn how to navigate. The geographical area was new, the people unfamiliar, and this time there was no family at my side. I did have co-workers who guided me through the process of getting car insurance, answered questions such as where to go to purchase household goods, etc. They did not know me and I did not know them, but I am grateful they were there. They were in fact, the only people I had to rely on aside from God. It was enough.

The first time I tried driving outside of Ramona to purchase some necessary household goods, I was told there was a Walmart in Poway where I could shop. Anything I could not purchase in our local Kmart, I purchased there. I remember trying to find my way back to Ramona and I made a wrong turn. I was so frightened. I had not yet learned how to use apps on the phone for navigation.

My GPS had given out, and I was lost. I finally found my way back, but I remember that I did not venture to go anywhere else but to church and Walmart for the first few months. I was too frightened of becoming lost once again.

Several months later a neighbor informed me there was a Target Store near the Walmart where I shopped. It was only a few short miles away and I did not know it! I could have had my choice of shopping experiences within a few short miles of each other. It sounds funny now, but not at the time. Strange that it would take me that long to make such a significant discovery. Fear had kept me isolated and afraid.

I remember another time I tried to brave it out and adventure a little bit further from Ramona. I became lost again. This time I was hopelessly lost, so when I finally found a seven eleven store, I stopped and tried to buy a map. They did not sell maps. I could not believe they had no maps for sale. So I tried to ask the clerks for directions; neither one could explain to me how to get back to Ramona. It seems strange even now. I can remember the fear that I felt. I do not know if I thought I would wind up in Mexico, the ocean, or what. It was not a reasonable fear, but I was afraid just the same.

A navigation system was necessary if I wanted to survive in this new territory. Although the money was not in the budget, I bought a new GPS. It had become as necessary as the food I ate. Without a system of navigation that I could rely on, I would not be able to acclimate myself in this brand new place. The GPS gave me a sense of freedom and safety that allowed me to not only acclimate, but adapt to my new surroundings.

While the geographical adjustment was difficult enough, the cultural adjustment was even harder. People in California, at least in the area I found myself in, do not relate to one another in quite the same way as we did in Ohio. People are more aloof and less friendly. I remember one church I attended for a period of months. Only three people even bothered to ask my name, and only one of them offered to eat lunch with me after church. Making friends and integrating myself into the social network seemed a daunting task.

I tried joining groups and becoming active in social organizations, and although it was initially helpful, the type of long term friendships I was looking for remained absent. I did not want invitations given out of a sense of obligation. I did not want to hang out with people who merely tolerated me because of the gifts they presumed I possessed, or because I was capable of performing a service which they desired. I wanted to find friends who celebrated my person, not just my gifts. Those friends are few and far between, but I have found a few. Once again, it was not easy; and it has taken years.

I remember not long ago, having a conversation about this very concern with one of my closest friends in California. I explained how hard it has been for me to make new friends. She said to me, Kathy you have to remember that the culture here is different than where you come from.

People in California rarely just hang out. Casual relationships are not like that here simply because of the hectic lifestyle we find ourselves engaged in. Time is tightly scheduled and structured. People interact by making plans in advance and scheduling it in on their calendar. Casually hanging out or going to lunch is not likely to happen. Do not take it personally; it is a part of living the fast paced lifestyle of a Californian.

By Ohio standards, I had been unsuccessful in integrating myself into the social environment. However, I am no longer in Ohio. The standards of social acceptance or rejection are no longer applicable because of where I am. I can no longer judge my success by the same measure I did back East. It is time to change the standards with which I measure success.

When driving in the United States, we measure distance by the US standard of a mile, but in other countries, that measure is far less common. The metric system is a more widely used system of measuring distance in countries outside of the US. The old adage is, when in Rome, do as the Romans do.

Even Paul stressed, "*...I have become all things to all men that I may by all means save some.*"

1 Corinthians 9:22b

He was talking of being adaptable to the people and surroundings you find yourself in at the time. Adaptability to the environment, the people, and the culture in a new territory are critical to a successful transition. This often requires a shift in one's mindset. I had to transition my thinking to develop a new mindset that will allow me to adapt to my new environment.

I can no longer expect or anticipate that relationships with friends or family will be quite the same as they were before I made the transition. All things have become new, and though new relationship standards are not necessarily better or worse, they are different. I no longer measure in the same way as I did before. I am adapting.

One must let go of the past before embracing the future.

Finally, we come to the next step in transition. It is the process of letting go of the past and embracing the future; putting down roots, accepting your new identity, and taking ownership of who you've become.

In many ways, it is a new day and a new beginning. Old things have passed away and all things have become new. You must be willing to allow the past to remain in the past and accept the new assignment with which God has commissioned you.

Just because it is the way you have always done things, it does not mean you continue to do the same. When advancing into new territory one must acclimate, adapt, establish and occupy. This is the formula for successfully transitioning into a new season of your life. You cannot always navigate by sight or sound, but you will hear a voice saying, this is the way. It is the voice of Wisdom, do you hear her speak? She will guide you along the unknown paths that you must walk in the future.

I learned that I would have to let go of past mindsets and past navigation systems, adopting the standards of living for where I have been planted. I have to embrace the new me and my new identity before the old me could be put to rest in the past. Having done so, I can now comfortably establish myself into the new environment in which I live. I can now safely move past survival mode to establishing a successful lifestyle in California.

I am reminded of a movie line that I am sure is familiar; Toto, we are not in Kansas anymore. That speaks to me. Kathy, you are not in Ohio any more. It is time to take off the old, put on the new, and become who God created me to be in the place he called me to do it. Acclimate, adapt, establish, and occupy; yes, I think it is time.

The Process of Successful Transition

Successfully transitioning from one season to the next, successfully transitioning from one territory into the next, takes time. The steps to a successful transition are:

1. acclimate
2. adapt to change
3. establish yourself in your new territory
4. occupy

What worked in the previous season may not work in the new. You may not be able to take the same habits, thought processes, and mindsets with you where you go. You may need to rely on a new means of navigation. You must be willing to adapt. You must be willing to change your mind set to be successful where you are going. Leaving behind the old and embracing the new is essential.

Some people that were close friends in the old season may need to remain behind. God will provide what you need where you are going. Just trust him. Allow the voice of wisdom to guide you as you establish yourself in the new place, and then occupy where you have been planted until further notice. Become who you were created to be, with God's help.

54

Chapter 6

Is Your Filter Clogged?

Have you ever had your furnace or air conditioner begin to wain in its performance, only to discover that the filter is clogged? I have. Without making certain the filter is kept clean, the heated or cooled air that flows through the filter becomes minimal and rendered ineffective. Peak performance demands a clean filter and it needs to be replaced or cleaned on a frequent basis to make certain it continues to be effective. Sometimes that same thing happens to our hearing. It becomes clogged up by life.

The many sights, sounds, and voices in our everyday life tend to drown out and cover up the one voice that we need to hear the most, the voice of wisdom. How can we effectively filter out the sound of life to hear her voice more clearly?

Filtering through the magnitude of sounds, noises, and voices first begins by learning to distinguish one from another. While the sound of the vacuum will never be confused with the sound of a family member's voice, they can both affect your ability to hear other sounds that are not as loud.

One key is the use of discernment. Discernment, not to be confused with the spiritual gift of discerning of spirits;[3] discernment is the ability to judge correctly between right and wrong. Discerning the sound of Wisdom's voice is a gift that one can develop with time and practice.

I have heard it said that an unborn baby has already learned the sound of its mother's voice and is able to discern it from the sound

---

[3] For more information on spiritual gifts, please refer to the author's book, *Treasures of the Heart, Gifts of the Trinity* written by Kathy Smith and published by Vision Publishing www.booksbyvision.com

of others; even before it actually sees the mother face to face. This is because the ability to distinguish one sound from another is developed through listening.

The more adept we become at recognizing the differences in voice tone and quality, the sooner we will be able to distinguish one voice from another. Mothers can often differentiate the sound of one child from another as a result of experience and familiarity. A mom knows the sound of her babies' voice. In addition she can often tell you why the baby is crying. There is the I'm bored cry, the cry of pain or hurt, or hunger. Sometimes the baby cries simply because it longs to have attention or to be held.

We too can learn to hear the voice of wisdom more clearly by listening for the tone, quality, and message of her voice. Solomon defined the characteristics of three women's voices, two of which he said to avoid. We know the message of Wisdom's voice will never contradict the word of God. Anything that does is not of him. What are some things that will clog up the filter to our hearing?

Wrong Mindsets

The victim mentality is a wrong mindset that blocks out the sound of truth. The fact that we are victors and not victims is often not heard by the one entrapped by this lie. The only way out is to dismiss the lie and embrace the truth. Your identity is in Christ and he is victorious, so you are victorious as well. Those who are entrapped in perpetual victimization may require professional help.[4] Victimization may happen to all of us at one time or another, but we do not need to live as victims. It is not an identity; it is not who we are but rather a circumstance we must walk through.

In addition to this wrong mindset, we have also mentioned a poverty mindset. Once again, this is a lie from the pit of hell that is in direct

---

[4] There is an excellent group of Christian counselors that belong to the organization IACCP. This is the International Association of Christian Counseling Professionals and for more assistance in this area you may request help at http://www.vision.edu/iaccp/

violation of the word of God. The word says, God shall supply all of our needs according to his riches in glory in Christ Jesus (Philippians 4:19). We all experience trials in the area of finances, but just because we are walking through a season it does not mean the season will go on forever. Seasons come and seasons go, unless you have not learned the biblical principles of stewardship.

Actually, any mindset that is contrary to the word of God can clog up our hearing of the truth. The only remedy for this is to hear and embrace truth. Replace the lies with what God's word says and keep hold of it. Do not rehearse the what if's that the enemy would speak in your ear. You shall know the truth and the truth shall set you free (John 8:32).

Just as the unborn baby comes to recognize the sound of the mother's voice through the intimate relationship that they both share, you too can know the sound of wisdom's voice through relationship. Relationship takes time and effort, it requires commitment. Are you willing to make the commitment to deepen your relationship, by acquiring knowledge and understanding? Are you willing to spend time in prayer, fellowship, and communion? That kind of commitment requires sacrifice, but not nearly the cost of the sacrifice he made for you. We have the mind of Christ (see 1 Corinthians 2:16). As a result of knowledge, understanding, and relationship we can discern the voice of wisdom speaking.

Chapter 7

Do You Hear Her Now?

Wisdom is more than knowledge, more than understanding; it is the ability to make sound judgements and develop divinely inspired plans that bring success in life. Navigating through the rough spots and pressing through the setbacks to discover the new day, and the new beginning.

Actually, each new day brings with it a brand new opportunity for success. Just think about it. If you messed up yesterday, last week, last year… you still have the opportunity to make it right in your today. This is indeed the day that the Lord has made, so let us rejoice and be glad in it (Psalm 118:24). Not everyone has the opportunity to get up in the morning and have a fresh start.

Some have gone on to be with the Lord, their hopes and dreams unfulfilled. That does not need to be your legacy. Today, you have a brand new opportunity to begin anew. Don't waste your fresh start. Listen, and listen carefully for the sound of her voice saying, "this is the way, walk in it."

If you find yourself unable to hear, it is time to begin examining why, because she is definitely speaking. Are you too busy with life in general to listen for her voice? Are there others that have caught your ear and your heart, drowning out the sound of her voice? Who are you listening to? Have you made time today to sit down and just listen?

Taking time to sit down and pray, meditate, and praise the Lord will awaken your ears to the sound of her voice. If you need to, get away to your own private place.

Have you seen the movie, War Room? Private time alone to sit, pray, and listen is key to gaining the knowledge, understanding, and wisdom you will need to walk out your day with success.

> *But if any of you lacks wisdom, let him ask of God, who gives to all generously and without reproach, and it will be given to him.*
>
> **James 1:5**

The wisdom you need to walk out your day, your week and your future is there for the taking, all you need to do is ask. Are you asking? Are you listening for the response? Do you hear her now?

Sometimes we become so caught up in life, we fail to remember what brought us to the Lord in the first place. It reminds me of a song from the past. Here are a few of the lyrics,

Try to remember the kind of September
When life was slow and oh, so mellow
Try to remember the kind of September
When grass was green and grain was yellow

Try to remember the kind of September
When you were a tender and callow fellow
Try to remember and if you remember then follow (follow)

Callow? The word means to be green as in a newbie. Do you remember when you were young in the Lord, a new believer? The lyrics go on,

Try to remember when life was so tender
That no one wept except the willow
Try to remember when life was so tender
That dreams were kept beside your pillow.

When you were young, you had time to dream about the future. Your future was bright and full of hope. You were in love; you were in love with God, because of who he is and what he has done. Do you remember what it was like when you first fell in love with the Lord?

The lyrics end like this:

*Deep in December, it's nice to remember
The fire of September that made us mellow
Try to remember and if you remember then follow.*

Can you follow your memories back to the beginning when all seemed bright and new? Can you follow them back to the first time you fell in love with God? Back to the time when you would spend time together and dream together endlessly? If you can, then follow. Remember and follow. [5]

Your first love is waiting to spend time with you again. Give yourself permission to hope again, dream again, love again as you did before, when you were callow. He is waiting with open arms, waiting for you to ask for the wisdom that you need. And if you ask, you shall receive, because Wisdom speaks.

---

[5] Inspired by an article published May 15, 2016 **"Try to Remember: Dream Again with Your First Love"** by Katherine Ruonala, Elijah List http://www.elijahlist.com/words/display_word.html?ID=16079

Wisdom

**Do Not Forsake Her,
And She Will Guard You;**

**Love Her,
And She Will Watch Over You.**

About the Author

Formerly from Ohio and North Carolina, Kathy now resides in Ramona, CA. She is an author, educator, and motivational speaker. She is a doctoral candidate at Vision International University and has an Associate's Degree in Nursing. She is an ordained minister with the Assemblies of God International Fellowship. She works as the Communications Director for Vision International University and is the Director of Vision Publishing. She is the Associate Publisher- Features for Faith Filled Family Magazine of Canada.

She is the author of Treasures *of the Heart* about the gifts of the Trinity, as well as this book, *Wisdom Speaks*. She is currently in the process of completing a *Guide for Effectual Pastoral Ministry* and a book on *Hospital Chaplaincy*.

For more information about Kathy and her ministry, you can go to www.planpurposedestiny.org or email her at ksmith@vision.edu

Recommended Resources

I Want To Be Like You Dad written by Dr. Stan DeKoven and available at www.booksbyvision.com

The Sound of His Voice written by Robert Nolan and available at www.booksbyvision.com

Treasures of the Heart Gifts Of The Trinity written by Kathy Smith and available at www.booksbyvision.com

Walk In Wisdom written by Dr. Stan DeKoven and available at www.booksbyvision.com

CPSIA information can be obtained
at www.ICGtesting.com
Printed in the USA
FSOW02n1623100816
23452FS